All the Right Moves

The Najee McGreen Story

By

Ron Berman

www.scobre.com

Scobre Press Corporation
2255 Calle Clara
La Jolla, CA 92037

Scobre Press books may be purchased for
educational, business or sales promotional use.

First Scobre edition published 2006.

Photography by Justin Smith, James Gunn & Kofi
McGreen
Edited by Helen Glenn Court
Cover Art & Layout by Michael Lynch

ISBN # 1-933423-61-7

HOME RUN EDITION
This story is based on the real life of Najee McGreen, although
some names, quotes, and details of events have been altered.

Chapter One

The Moment

The year was 1993, and America was changing. A young governor from Arkansas, Bill Clinton, had just been elected president. Rap stars Snoop Dogg and Dr. Dre were climbing the music charts. *Jurassic Park* was the top movie of the year, earning millions of dollars. The Sony PlayStation had been released. In sports, Michael Jordan was leading the Chicago Bulls to the NBA championship. The Dallas Cowboys had just won the Super Bowl.

The changing face of America could best be seen from the streets of "The Big Apple." New York City has always been the center of sports, politics, and entertainment. In the early 1990s, a man named David Dinkins was serving as mayor. He was the first African American in the city's history to hold that office. Mayor Dinkins had won the election by defeating Rudy Giuliani. One day Mr. Giuliani would also be elected mayor.

Times Square in New York City: fast-paced and exciting.

During that same year, 1993, many things were happening. A producer from New York was forming a new record company. His name was Sean "Puffy" Combs, and he was twenty-four years old. He named his new company Bad Boy Records. Soon, Puffy's main artist, Notorious B.I.G., became a big star.

Superstars—in all fields—seem to have something in common. It's like a fire that burns brightly inside them. They are determined to achieve their goals. These people work hard to develop their skills. They refuse to give up until they come out on top. In New York, that's known as "making it big."

In 1993, things were also starting to happen for a young man named Najee McGreen. One day he would also be "making it big." Najee lived in a small house in the Bushwick neighborhood of Brooklyn.

Although he was only five years old, this star was already beginning to shine…

"Whatcha' doing, Dad?" Najee asked, walking into the kitchen. In his hand was a toy train that he had built with Legos. Najee was always playing with Legos. He loved building things and pretending they were real.

Najee's father, Kofi McGreen, was sitting at the kitchen table. After a long day at work, he was relaxing with a hot cup of coffee. He was reading a magazine. Mr. McGreen smiled, placing his young son up on his lap. "I'm reading an article about a game called chess. I've never actually played it, but it sounds like fun."

Najee looked at the magazine, which had a color photo of a chessboard. The black and white pieces looked really cool. Mr. McGreen saw that Najee was interested, so he started reading aloud from the magazine. The article talked about the history of chess and how the game is played. As his father spoke, Najee couldn't stop staring at the photo of the chessboard. He was drawn to it in a way that was impossible to explain.

Mr. McGreen told Najee that chess is a game of strategy. Pieces are allowed to move in specific ways. For example, a pawn can only move forward. It happens to be the least important piece on the board. The knight is the one piece that is allowed to jump over other pieces. The object of chess is to move

3

pieces forward. Along the way, a player tries to capture his opponent's pieces. Finally, a player tries to corner and trap his opponent's king. When a king is trapped and has nowhere to move, this is known as checkmate. That's how a player wins the game.

A game of chess is a tough battle, similar to a war. However, there are no tanks, long-range missiles, B-52 Bombers, or hand grenades. Chess is a game that is played with the *mind*.

Najee had been listening carefully as his father spoke. With a determined look on his face, he asked, "Can we play?"

"Sure, follow me," Mr. McGreen replied with a smile. He seemed to remember that he had once been given a chessboard as a gift. He wondered if it might be in the closet, along with the other board games.

Mr. McGreen reached up to the top shelf of the closet. He pulled down the Scrabble set, the Monopoly board, and a deck of cards. Finally, he found what he was looking for. Blowing the dust off a brand new, tiny chess set, he handed it down to Najee. Taking off like a rocket, Najee ran to the living room and began opening the game. Mr. McGreen laughed and joined his son.

Fifteen minutes later, Mr. McGreen was trying to understand the directions. He had set the board up with the pieces in the correct positions. Finally, he started reading aloud. He explained what each piece was called and how it was allowed to move. Najee, meanwhile, stared at the chessboard like it was a long-lost friend. As his father spoke, Najee nodded his head. He just *understood*.

It's not hard to imagine Derek Jeter holding a bat in his hand for the first time. Picture Spike Lee looking through his first camera lens . . . or Peyton Manning tossing his first pass. Like Tiger Woods ripping his very first drive, or Oprah conducting her first interview, another natural—Najee McGreen—was holding a chess piece in his hand for the first time.

"This is my move," Najee declared, pushing the white pawn forward.

Mr. McGreen said, "That's a very good opening move, Najee. Okay, my turn." He took one of his black pawns out from its starting position and advanced it forward. He picked up the directions so that he could help Najee make his next move. Before he could say anything, though, Najee made another move.

"Hold on, Najee. I'm not sure you're allowed to move that piece there," Mr. McGreen said. Looking at the directions, he was shocked to find out that Najee's move was legal. It was also a very good move. "How did you know to do that?"

"I don't know," Najee answered. "It just seemed to make sense to bring my knight out to protect the pawn." Mr. McGreen had explained the rules to Najee one time only. That was all it had taken. Najee had listened, and remembered them.

One of the earliest photos of Najee playing chess.

Mr. McGreen shook his head and smiled. Using the directions as a guide, he made his next move. Again, Najee wasted no time before making another move. Mr. McGreen couldn't believe it. How could a five-year-old be so good at a complicated game he had just learned? It simply didn't make sense.

Mr. McGreen would soon find out the answer to this question. This had been the moment when greatness first showed itself. It's likely that every star has a "moment" at some point in his or her life. For Najee McGreen, this was that moment.

But moments come and go. There are no short-cuts to success. Having a dream is a great beginning. After that, it's all about dedication, determination, and hard work—that's what "making it big" is all about.

With the passing years, Najee found himself in the winner's circle time and time again. But that was just the beginning ... he would also win awards for his business accomplishments, and even appear on the cover of magazines.

Chapter Two

Chess Competition

"C'mon, Najee, we have to leave or we'll be late." Mr. McGreen checked his watch. He was holding a bright blue flyer that read: *Celebrate Kwanzaa at Malcolm X Elementary School. Come play in our Kwanzaa Chess Tournament. All ages welcome!*

Kwanzaa is a traditional holiday observed by African Americans. It's a celebration that takes place over the final week of each year. Established in 1966, it honors African American heritage. Malcolm X Elementary School was holding the chess tournament as part of its Kwanzaa celebration.

Najee carefully put away the train he was building with Legos. He ran down the hallway to the front door. The McGreens lived in a small, comfortable brick house. Luckily, it was big enough for their family, which was growing. It now included Najee's little brother, Jabari, who was only a year old.

The McGreen family, summer of 2006: Mr. and Mrs. McGreen, flanked by sons Jabari and Najee, with daughters Maya and Mariah.

Najee kissed his mother goodbye and softly patted his baby brother's head. He and his father walked to the bus stop and boarded the B-26 bus. The McGreens lived in Brooklyn, which is one of the five boroughs of New York City. The other four are Manhattan, the Bronx, Queens, and Staten Island. With more than 2 million residents, Brooklyn has more people than the four other boroughs.

Fifteen minutes later, Mr. McGreen and Najee arrived at Malcolm X Elementary School. When they entered the large gym, they looked around in awe. There were ten tables set up with chessboards. This was Najee's first experience at a chess tournament. It was a little bit intimidating.

The five boroughs of New York City.

"Just have fun and do the best you can," Mr. McGreen said. He realized that Najee was nervous. "It's less than a year since you played chess for the first time. No pressure, it doesn't matter if you win or lose."

These words from his father calmed Najee down. Mr. McGreen was expecting Najee to do well, though. It all started the first time they had played chess. Since then, it was clear that Najee had a lot of ability. Within weeks he was playing complete games. He was learning more about chess all the time.

Najee, like a lot of kids, had been blessed with

talent. What made him different was that his talent made him work harder. Many talented young people get bored easily. Sometimes they don't work very hard. Later, they wonder how things might have turned out if they had tried harder. People who push themselves almost always end up becoming successful. Some of them even turn out to be superstars.

Najee, doing a little reading, catches some sleep on a giant book.

Najee had come into the Kwanzaa tournament hoping he would win some of his games. As it turned out, he had nothing to worry about. This was a small chess tournament. Nobody in his age group could compete with him. Najee defeated all of his opponents with ease. He won the first chess competition he had ever entered. His reward was a three-inch trophy. It was *tiny*. At that moment, though, Najee felt like he was holding an Olympic gold medal.

On the bus ride home, Najee couldn't take his eyes off the trophy. He couldn't wait to run inside his house and show it to his mother. The feeling of winning was awesome. It made him want to compete again as soon as possible. Najee started thinking about the next tournament. He had every reason to think that he would win once again.

The trophy may not be huge, but the feeling of accomplishment sure is ... Najee and his father celebrate.

A month later, Najee and his father headed to PS 9. In New York, many public schools are identified with PS (public school) and a number. PS 9 was located on the Upper East Side, a neighborhood in Manhattan. To get there, they took the C-train up to

86th street. Beneath the streets of New York City is a complicated maze of trains and tunnels. Millions of passengers use them to get to school, work, and other places.

The subway ride from Brooklyn had taken almost an hour. Najee and his father came out from the underground train. They were on the way to Najee's second chess tournament. They walked back two blocks to 84th street, where the school was located. It was a cold and breezy day. The wind nearly blew Najee's cap off his head.

Unlike the tournament at Malcolm X Elementary School, this was a rated tournament. This meant that excellent junior players would be playing. The fee to play was $30. That was a lot of money, but Mr.

McGreen felt that it was worth it. After all, Najee was very excited about the tournament.

Najee's first game was against a kid named Will Gibson. Although they were the same age, Will was bigger than Najee. He was also very cocky. He had been playing chess tournaments for more than a year. Because of that, he had a lot more experience than Najee.

"Who are you?" Will asked with a sarcastic look on his face before they played. "I've never seen you at any tournaments before. Is this your first one?"

"Nope, I won the Kwanzaa tournament at Malcolm X Elementary," Najee replied proudly. To his surprise, Will started laughing out loud.

"Did you hear that, Chris?" Will said, turning to his friend, who was watching. "It sounds like little Najee won a *really* important tournament." As Chris laughed, Najee became embarrassed.

Will may have been a punk, but he certainly knew how to play chess. That became obvious almost as soon as the game started. He made a combination of moves that Najee had never seen before. Najee was confused. He didn't realize that Will was laying a trap for him. Good chess players can make moves and then guess what their opponents will do. So they plan ahead. Great chess players can plan out several moves in advance—in their head.

After twenty moves, Najee was in big trouble. Will had already captured two of his best pieces. Najee was getting his first taste of real chess competition. By the time the game was over, Will had handed Najee a crushing defeat.

Luckily, Najee wasn't out of the tournament. The rules were no-elimination, so he still had three other games to play. He was sure that he would get back on the winning track. But this was a high-level tournament. Najee simply wasn't in the same class as the rest of the field. It ended up being a humiliating afternoon. Najee lost all four games he played. None of them were even close.

When it was all over, Najee gathered his coat and walked out with his father. His head was down. As they walked to the train, he didn't say a word. Mr. McGreen wondered if Najee's interest in chess might go away.

Not a chance. There was a reason Najee was

quiet and walking with his head down. It wasn't because he was upset or discouraged. Sure, it had been embarrassing to lose all four games. That didn't matter, though. As he walked along with his father, Najee was replaying the games in his mind. He was trying to understand how those other kids had beaten him so easily. Najee wanted to figure out the strategy they had used.

Najee wasn't quitting the game. His confidence may have been shaken, but he was determined to fight back. He had already experienced the joy of winning in the first tournament. That made him hungry to improve. Now, losing made him even hungrier.

Failure causes some people to give up. Successful people, on the other hand, always bounce back. They find out that hard times make them even stronger. Clearly, Najee had this quality. It was helpful on a day when his chess dreams came crashing down. It would also prove valuable many years later. It was one of the reasons Najee would win awards for his skill with computers. It would also help him run a successful business by the age of *fifteen*.

Mr. McGreen and Najee walked down the steps into the subway on 86th street. Mr. McGreen tried to cheer up his son, "Hey, Najee, how would you like to go get some ice cream? We can go home and watch a movie and. . . "

Najee looked up at his father before he could finish his sentence. Najee was fired up. "No thanks,

Dad, I'm not hungry. I want to get home and get out the chessboard. I have a ton of work to do."

Working hard to improve: Najee plays with Watu, a National Master from South Africa on his first trip to the United States. Afterwards, smiles all around.

Chapter Three

Chess Hustlers
and Wall Street Executives

As the years rolled on, Najee McGreen became even more involved with chess. In addition to playing with his father, he started taking lessons. Najee's teacher, Alexander, taught him many new things.

Najee's parents were amazed by their son's devotion to the game. As his skills developed, Najee started to win tournaments. There was no doubt that the chess lessons had helped. Although Alexander was strict, he was the perfect teacher for Najee. He believed that chess should be a quiet and "proper" game.

He wasn't alone. Chess has always been that way. It's not like a basketball or football game, where fans are going crazy. There's no music, and no cheerleaders on the sidelines. At chess tournaments, the applause is usually quiet and serious. It's not too often that fans get loud and excited.

Najee collects his first place trophy at the Philadelphia World Open in 1996.

The game of chess has been around for a long time, well over a thousand years. It is believed that chess may have first appeared in India. In the United States, it has become more and more popular over the years. The USCF (United States Chess Federation) was founded in 1939. It has more than 80,000 members.

Although chess was a quiet game, there was one spot where it was just the opposite. Washington Square Park was located in the Greenwich Village neighborhood of Manhattan. The park was surrounded by world famous NYU (New York University).

People would show up every day at Washington Square Park. They would come to put their chess skills to the test. Along West 4th Street, set against the shady oak trees, were several chessboards. Chess hustlers and Wall Street executives would play chess—usually for money.

One day, Najee's father took him to Washington Square Park. It wasn't a planned trip. Mr. McGreen and Najee had been in Manhattan for a junior chess tournament. After going out for lunch, they were on the way home.

Mr. McGreen realized that they were just a few blocks from Washington Square Park. He smiled and turned away from the subway station. Instead of heading back to Brooklyn, he and Najee walked to the park. When they arrived, they went over to the area where the chess tables were located.

It was an amazing sight. There were stone tables built into the ground, with chessboards covering the tabletops. Every table was being used. Najee couldn't believe what he was seeing. People of all ages and skill levels were playing chess. It wasn't quiet like a tournament. Instead, it was noisy and exciting. People were talking, laughing, swearing, and cheering—even as the games were being played!

Through the years, some amazing chess players have come to Washington Square Park. As a matter of fact, Bobby Fischer got his start there. Many people believe that he is the greatest chess player in history.

Najee poses with International Chess Master Josh Waitzkin, who was the inspiration for the movie *Searching for Bobby Fischer*.

Born in Chicago in 1943, Bobby Fischer was an eight-time United States champion. Despite his success, his life has always been strange. It started after he won the World Chess Championship in 1972. He dropped out of sight for much of the next twenty years. The chess world—and Hollywood—has always found him interesting. That's why a movie was made, titled *Searching for Bobby Fischer*.

As a chess fan, Najee knew all about Bobby Fischer. He was excited to be in the same spot where Fischer had once played. Looking around, Najee saw that there were many different types of people playing chess. They were all here because they loved the game. There were construction workers, students, and street people.

An interesting type of chess was played at Washington Square Park. Known as speed chess, a clock was an important part of the action. Each player was limited to a set amount of time. Other than losing by checkmate, a player could also lose by using too much time. In speed chess, games were ten minutes long.

Playing quickly and under pressure leads to mistakes. This makes speed chess a true test of skill. Najee didn't have a lot of experience playing speed chess. Still, he wanted to square off against the "regulars" who hung out at the park. His father put a five-dollar bill down on the table. Soon, Najee was playing his first game. He was matched up against Rick Duhon, a hippie with long blonde hair.

This is the type of clock used in speed chess—it has dual timers, one for each player.

A large crowd gathered around the table to watch. To their surprise, Najee destroyed Mr. Duhon in twenty-four quick moves. As they shook hands, the crowd suddenly parted. Najee's next opponent was coming through.

The man was tall, wearing a brown coat and a cap turned backwards. Everybody started whispering when Willie Foster sat down across from Najee. He smelled of beer and had a thin cigar hanging off the corner of his mouth. Willie looked at his opponent—who was about thirty years younger than he was.

Willie made his living hustling young Wall Street executives in chess. He had twenty-five years of experience playing speed chess. This veteran player understood the fine points of the game inside out.

After Mr. McGreen put down another five-dollar bill, the clocks were set. The game started, and so did Willie's trash talking. He joked that it was getting close to Najee's *nap time*. He also declared that a little kid wasn't taking down the famous *Willie Foster*.

Trash talking aside, the main event was the chess. Eight moves into the game, Willie made a mistake—or so it seemed. He brought out his knight, leaving himself open to attack. Najee knew that he had to move quickly because of the time limit. So, without thinking about it, he captured Willie's knight. With a grin, Willie attacked from a different angle with his queen.

It only took a few moves for Najee to realize what had happened. Willie, using an unusual strategy, had set a trap for his young opponent. Najee had fallen right into it. He was in big trouble.

The crowd whispered that the game was over. Willie smiled and eased back in his seat. Suddenly, though, Najee saw a possible opening. It would be risky, but he quickly decided that he had nothing to lose. In his mind, he planned out his next five moves.

Seeing a chessboard in your head is a very difficult thing to do. After all, it shifts with every single move. The board has sixty-four individual squares. At the start of a game, each player has sixteen pieces. So the possibilities are endless. That's why it was such an advantage that Najee could picture the board in his head. This was a skill he had in common with great chess players.

The crowd started yelling with excitement as several moves were suddenly made. When Najee captured Willie's rook—one of the most valuable pieces on the board—everybody gasped. Small beads of sweat rolled down Willie's forehead. Now *he* was in a jam.

"Chess is so cool," Najee explains. "Things can change in an instant. Sometimes you almost feel like you're in a boxing match. Even though you sit there quietly, it's like you're trading punches with your opponent. Your heart is pounding and your mind is racing. It's very intense."

This game was going right down to the wire. Less than thirty seconds remained on the clock! At this point, both players were making moves at blazing speed. Finally, though, the more experienced player won. With a fantastic move, Willie Foster pulled the game out. The crowd applauded and cheered for both players.

Willie stood up and took the five-dollar bill,

which he had won fair and square. He turned to his friends in the crowd. There was a lot of yelling and high-fives. Willie was definitely enjoying the attention.

Meanwhile, Najee quietly got up and turned around, preparing to leave with his father. Suddenly, he felt a hand on his shoulder. Willie leaned in close to him and whispered, "Kid, you did yourself proud today. You're the best young player I've seen here in a long time."

Then, very quickly, Willie shoved the five-dollar bill into Najee's hand. Before Najee could even respond, Willie turned away and walked back into the crowd.

Najee never spent that five-dollar bill. He still has it today—it reminds him of the day he earned respect from Willie Foster.

To be the best, you need a lot of experience. In addition to playing against Willie Foster, Najee has also had the opportunity to play against the best in the world! Above, he competes against Garry Kasparov, chess Grandmaster and former world champion, during an exhibition chess event. Below, Najee recently battled it out with International Grandmaster Maurice Ashley.

Chapter Four

The Magic of Computers

It was the year 2000, four years after Najee played chess in Washington Square Park. Najee was twelve years old. One day he was at home, busy as always. He didn't even hear as Jabari called out, "Najee, dinner." Getting no response, Najee's seven-year-old brother walked down to the basement. Upstairs, Mrs. McGreen was getting one-year-old twins Maya and Mariah ready for bed.

Coming down the stairs, Jabari saw Najee standing over a computer. He held a small flashlight in his mouth and a screwdriver in his right hand. "Hey, Najee, what are you doing?" Jabari asked.

"I've just finished replacing the hard drive on this one," Najee answered proudly. He screwed the back cover shut. "Let's see if it works."

Najee had spent close to a week working on this computer. He had been so busy that he didn't even have time to hang out with his friends. Najee pushed the "on" button. Within minutes the Windows desktop appeared on the screen. "Yes!" he exclaimed.

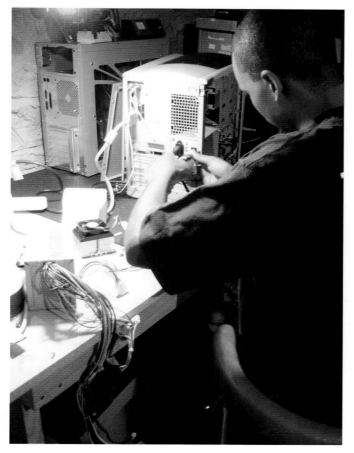

Najee fixes a computer.

Computers were Najee's new hobby. Of course, he was still a competitive chess player. The trophy case in his bedroom had more than fifty trophies! Najee had become one of the best junior chess players in New York.

There were many benefits to being an excellent chess player. One of them was the opportunity to travel. Najee and his family had been all over the United States at chess tournaments. One of his best memories was a huge tournament in Tucson, Arizona. It was called the Great Days and Knights National Chess Tournament.

Najee, right, with some friends, on the way to a tournament several years ago.

The McGreens arrived in Tucson, where the temperature outside was 105 degrees. Mr. McGreen and Najee went over to the event center, where the tournament was being held. Najee had been to many tournaments, but this was special. "It was the most chess players I had ever seen at one time," he remembers. "I was pretty pumped up."

Najee checked the list posted on the wall. He saw that more than 500 kids had entered—in his age division alone! They were listed in order of their rating. Unfortunately, Najee was down at 150. That meant that 149 kids were expected to finish ahead of him. Trophies would be awarded to the top twenty-five only, so Najee faced a big challenge.

Junior chess in the United States is very competitive. There are thousands of local chess tournaments. There are also a handful of national tournaments that carry the most weight. This tournament, in Tucson, was extremely important.

Najee checked in and waited nervously until his first match was set to begin. When it was time, he went into the huge playing area—alone. Parents were not allowed inside while the competition was taking place. The only adults in the room were the tournament directors. This allowed kids to compete without the pressure of parents watching them.

An hour later, Najee came outside. He reported to his father that he had won his first game. This was a major opportunity for him. It wasn't going to be easy, however. Now that he was in the second round, the competition was about to get tougher.

Early in his next game, Najee "hung" his rook. In chess, that means accidentally leaving a piece unprotected. His rook was captured right away. This was a big problem. Without it, Najee was in real trouble. He played on, but he was a little bit shaken.

Najee shakes the hand of an opponent. He always displays good sportsmanship, win or lose.

The next hour passed slowly. Mr. McGreen wondered what was happening inside the playing area. As other games ended, kids were coming out to be with their families. But still, no Najee. This first day of competition was going down to the wire. Najee and his opponent were the last two competitors inside.

Finally, Najee came outside. Sweat was rolling down his face and he looked very tired. Unable to speak, he sat down in a chair next to his father. Mr. McGreen, thinking that Najee had lost, put his arm around his son's shoulder. He said, "I'm sorry, but great effort anyway."

Finding his voice, Najee turned to his dad. With a big smile on his face, he said, "Don't be sorry. I won, I'm moving on to the next round!"

Najee ended up placing thirtieth out of the entire field. He had started the tournament as number 150, so this was a fantastic performance. He was proud of himself for doing so well.

Besides chess, Najee had discovered another hobby. Personal computers were becoming popular at the time. Najee found out about a computer genius named Bill Gates. The name of his company was Microsoft. Mr. Gates had followed his dreams in the field of computers and software. Less than twenty years later, he had become the richest man in the world!

The first time Najee saw the magic of computers was at a chess tournament. It was being held at a private school in a nice Manhattan neighborhood.

Spectacular: the Manhattan skyline.

Najee and his father were walking down the hallway to get a soda. Najee was amazed by what he saw on the walls. There was computer artwork, and homework assignments that had been typed out. It was obvious that students at this school did much of their work on computers.

"Dad, how come all these. . . "

"This is a private school, Najee. Families pay money to send their kids to school here. That means that this school has enough money to buy computers for them to use. These kids probably have computers at home as well."

Najee was only eleven years old at the time. Still, he understood what his father was telling him. Najee had always known that there were advantages to being rich. But now he realized that one of the advantages was education.

Najee wasn't angry that some kids had it easier than others. He knew that no matter what, he could make his dreams come true. It didn't matter where he started. It was where he finished that would count.

After losing in his first real chess tournament, Najee had worked even harder. Now, he would have to do it again. He would have to outwork these kids. That's what the American dream was all about. It was within his reach. Najee just *knew* it.

There was something else he knew. Computers were the key. Najee needed to get a computer. His family couldn't afford it at the time, but he told himself: *I have to make it happen as soon as possible*. All he needed was an opportunity.

The opportunity came less than one year later. Najee's school hired someone named Stephen to come and build a computer. The school didn't have much money, so it wasn't going to be a fancy computer. Still, it was very exciting. Every day at school, Najee watched Stephen take spare parts and put them all together. Stephen explained to Najee how everything worked.

The day finally came that Stephen screwed the top back on the computer tower. As he turned the machine on, Najee's heart was racing. He hoped it would work. When the desktop appeared on the screen, it was an awesome feeling. Najee's school finally had a computer.

Najee began planning his next step: building a computer of his own, at home. Over the next couple of months, he continued to learn more about computers. He checked out library books, and did online research using the computer at school. Najee didn't have money for the parts he would need. Still, that didn't stop him from studying this exciting new field.

One night, Najee had an interesting idea. With summer approaching, he thought about skipping camp. He knew that, every year, his parents would set money aside for camp. Over dinner, he asked them a question: what if they used the camp money to buy spare computer parts instead?

Mr. and Mrs. McGreen couldn't believe that Najee was willing to skip camp. At first, they were against the idea. But after seeing the determination in his eyes, they finally agreed.

That summer turned out to be the busiest of Najee's life. He spent all his free time on his new project. At the beginning, he wondered if he would be able to do it. When Najee was finally finished, the computer worked! It was one of the most satisfying moments of his life.

Najee now had a computer and the Internet at his fingertips. He started chatting online with other chess players, and learning about new software. These skills would come in handy as he continued along his journey.

As time goes on, Najee continues to expand his knowledge. He is shown here, hanging out with a friend as they fix a computer together.

Chapter Five

A Wrong Move

As time went on, Najee became more and more involved with computers. Like most kids, he also loved video games. His first gaming system was the Sega Genesis. It featured the popular games *Sonic* and *Mortal Kombat*.

The Atari and Nintendo systems had been the first to become popular in the United States. The graphics and game play of the Sega Genesis was an upgrade. Still, it wasn't even close to the sounds and graphics of modern systems. Compared with a system such as Xbox 360, the Sega Genesis was very basic.

Najee came across an interesting article on the Internet one day. It talked about how much money was involved with computer and video games. Najee discovered that it's a huge business. Thousands of people work in the computer and video game business. Games earn billions of dollars in sales every year.

They have made superstars out of people such as John Madden. His game *John Madden Football* has been a bestseller for years.

Even though games were fun, they once put Najee in a dangerous position. He ended up being taught a worthwhile lesson. "I didn't really think about it at the time," he says. "But I realized later that it could have been a game-over type of mistake."

Najee's interest in video games goes way back.

In the game of chess, one wrong move can end your chance of winning. It's no different out there in the real world. With just one wrong move, things can take a tragic turn for the worse. That's why it's important to stay focused, stay smart, and make good decisions.

One day Najee was sitting on a bench at the Wilson Avenue station. He was waiting for the L train. Najee, an honor student, was attending middle school in Manhattan at the time. He traveled there every morning from his home in Brooklyn. The trip included the L train and the 6 train. It took over an hour each way.

As always, Najee had his Game Boy with him. He took it everywhere he went. It was fun, and it helped pass the time while he waited for the train. Of course, he knew that there was risk carrying something valuable while riding the subway. His parents had warned him many times. They told him what to do if he were ever robbed.

"Give them whatever they want and then call the police. Don't try to be a hero," Mr. and Mrs. McGreen said. To prove their point, they told him a true story about a murder. Tragically, it had taken place after a gold chain had been snatched. That incident had happened at this very same station—the Wilson Avenue station.

It wasn't just adult criminals that Najee's parents were worried about. They knew that many kids had given up on the American dream. Some of these kids weren't much older than Najee. Sadly, they had already traded in their schoolbooks for knives, guns, and drugs.

The high school dropout rate across America is shocking. It is believed that as many as 30 percent of kids don't graduate every year. It's worse in New York, where up to 40 percent of kids don't graduate.

Life is complicated, no matter what. But it's even more difficult when teenagers fail to get a high school diploma. They are setting themselves up for disappointment. They find out quickly that without an education, the world is unkind to them. Dropping out of school—their first bad choice—can have a domino effect. In many cases, it leads to even worse choices. The likely outcome is jail, poverty, and according to the statistics, even violent death.

Najee was lucky, because he had active and involved parents. Their influence had made an enormous difference. Many kids don't have that type of advantage. Still, there are great role models who should inspire them to pursue their dreams. Most kids in New York City have heard about successful people who came from their neighborhoods. Many of those talented people grew up in difficult situations. None of them came from fancy penthouses on Park Avenue.

One example is business leader Russell Simmons. A native of Queens, Mr. Simmons has an estimated net worth of $500 million. He is the owner of Def Jam Records. Not long ago he sold his clothing company *Phat Farm* for more than $100 million.

That's just the beginning. Jennifer Lopez rose out of the Bronx to become a superstar singer, dancer, and actress. And how about Howard Schultz, who started a little coffee joint called Starbucks? Mr. Schultz, a Brooklyn native, is now reportedly worth $700 million. He started small and ended up growing one of the largest businesses in the world.

Najee was sitting in the station with his backpack on his shoulders. He was completely zoned in on his Game Boy. He was trying to beat his own record in the game *Tetris*. For a moment, he almost didn't care that the train was late.

Najee's backpack felt heavy. It was filled with schoolbooks and some parts he had bought for his computer. Things had changed ever since Najee built that first computer. He had learned more and more about technology. He was actually becoming an expert. He knew how to repair computers and download cool new software. People around the neighborhood were even starting to ask for his help.

Pressing pause, Najee turned his head to look for the train. At that instant, an older kid came up to him and asked what time it was. Najee didn't think anything of it—even as the kid was staring at Najee's Game Boy.

Suddenly, with a violent gesture, the other kid grabbed the Game Boy. He yanked it free from Najee's hands and ran in the other direction. He hopped on a train that had just arrived. This was not the train that Najee had been waiting for. However, without thinking, Najee jumped to his feet and hopped on the train.

It was like a scene out of a movie. The older

boy ran quickly from car to car, with Najee chasing him. Luckily, an undercover police officer was on the train. He saw what was happening and immediately stopped both boys. Najee eventually got his Game Boy back. First, though, he and the other kid were taken to the police station.

Najee believes in the rule of law. That's why it was a wake-up for him when he ended up at the police station.

This had been a very dangerous situation. Not because of what happened, but because of what *might* have happened. What if the undercover police officer hadn't been there? What if the thief Najee was chasing had been carrying a knife or a gun?

It wasn't much different than the story Najee had been told about the murder. That had happened at this very same station. In that instance, it was a gold chain; here it was a Game Boy. Still, the result could have been the same. All of Najee's talent, and all of his hard work, could have been wasted in a second. All for a Game Boy.

Najee sat on a cold metal chair in the police station. He was waiting for his mother to get down there to pick him up. Najee looked around. There was a lot of activity taking place. Computers, naturally, were the focus. Secretaries were typing out information. Investigators were using the Internet to log into a special government Web site. That was helping them follow up on leads, and check whether suspects had prior convictions.

Seeing this new technology all around him had a big impact on Najee at that moment. For him, computers represented a brand new world. They were exciting, and there was no limit to what they could do. An important shift in Najee's life had begun. Like chess, it would lead him down an incredible road.

Yet, Najee had almost thrown it all away. He placed his head in his hands. He realized that he had taken his eye off the ball. Did a Game Boy really matter? Najee had stupidly let something threaten what he was trying to achieve. "I should have just let it slide," he says. "While it was happening, my instinct told me not to be a punk. I didn't want him to get away with my property. But chasing that kid could have ended up being the last thing I ever did."

Najee is right. He learned a valuable lesson about life that day: sometimes avoiding a *wrong* move is just as important as making a right move.

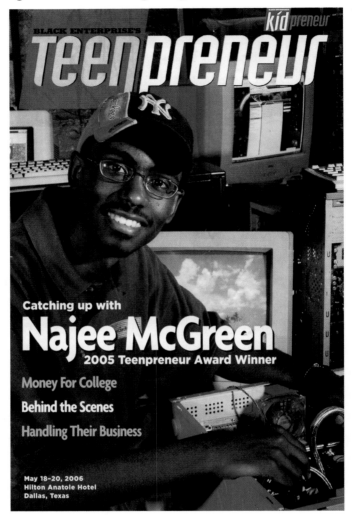

All the right moves: one part of success is learning from mistakes, and continuing down the right path. This formula has worked out well for Najee. As a matter of fact, three years later, he would be featured on the cover of a magazine!

Chapter Six

Techmaster Computer Works

Not long after the Game Boy incident, Najee's business career began to take off. He had become known as the neighborhood computer "fix-it" kid. Whenever somebody's computer needed repair, they knew who to call. This was perfect for Najee. He was gaining experience solving problems and working on computers.

One day, a different type of opportunity opened up for Najee. He was scheduled to play in a chess tournament in Manhattan. When he arrived, he found out that the tournament director had gotten sick. Nobody was there to run the event. Najee was interested. He knew that the job involved a computer program that he was familiar with.

A tournament director combines chess knowledge with computer skill. He is responsible for organizing the event and arranging the times of each match. He also determines which players should square off against each other.

As a thirteen-year-old chess champion, Najee had already won plenty of tournaments. He wondered how it would feel to be on the other side—actually running a tournament. This was an interesting new challenge. So, Najee volunteered to become the tournament director.

The sponsor of the tournament was an organization called The Right Move Chess Foundation. Fred Goldhirsch was the chairman of the organization. He agreed to give Najee the opportunity. Mr. Goldhirsch, who had known Najee for many years, was one of his biggest supporters. He had great faith in Najee's potential.

Najee and his mentor, Fred Goldhirsch, enjoy a game of tennis.

Najee did a first-rate job. He showed patience and understanding with players and their parents. Together with his computer skills, he was a natural for the position. Everybody said that the tournament ran smoothly with Najee in charge.

Tournament director Najee reviews the schedule.

While all of this was going on, The Right Move Chess Foundation had a meeting. They decided to upgrade their Web site. Up to that point, it had been a basic one-page layout. It simply gave general information about the organization. Seeing Najee's computer skills, Mr. Goldhirsch hired him as a Web designer. Najee's job was to improve the Web site of The Right Move Chess Foundation.

This was a good opportunity for a thirteen-year-old kid. A future career as a Web designer didn't sound bad at all. A top Web designer can earn up to $100 an hour! Najee had been hired by a real business to do a very important job. Peter, one of his friends, gave him a copy of the computer program *Dreamweaver.* This was a program used to build Web sites.

Najee couldn't believe his luck. Building Web sites was something he had thought about for a long time. This was a chance to jump right in. For the next three weeks, he hardly ever came out of his room. He was experimenting with the computer program and learning it inside out. Just as with chess and repairing computers, Najee's hard work paid off.

That summer, Najee built a brand new Web site for The Right Move Chess Foundation. He showed it to Mr. Goldhirsch at a meeting in a big conference room. Najee, wearing a suit and tie, tried to look as professional as possible. He was definitely nervous. As it turned out, he had nothing to worry about. Mr. Goldhirsch loved the site! Najee was immediately put in charge of the Web site. He was also asked to serve as tournament director for several more chess events.

By the time Najee was in the eighth grade, he was ready for another challenge. He was already acing tests in school, but that wasn't enough for him. So, Najee founded his company, Techmaster Computer Works.

That's right, *his* company. Techmaster Computer Works is a company that Najee McGreen founded at the age of only fourteen. He was already having success repairing computers and designing Web sites. At first he had done it for free, happy to gain the experience. Later, he decided to turn it into a real business and charge people. Techmaster Computer Works was born. Najee eventually designed a cool Web site for it: www.techmastercomputerworks.com.

Techmaster Computer Works was a small business at first. One day it would grow and lead to bigger things. That wasn't due to happen for a couple of years, though. First, Najee completed the eighth grade and moved on to high school.

In 2002, Najee was a freshman in high school, at Benjamin Banneker Academy in Brooklyn. Before that, he had attended middle school in Manhattan. It was nice to return to Brooklyn for high school. Najee didn't have to spend time traveling to and from Manhattan. This was more convenient, and it also made it easier for him to run his business.

Unfortunately, the switch to high school was tough for Najee. This was not unusual. A lot of kids have trouble adjusting to a new school, older kids, and harder classes. Najee's situation was different, though. Teachers kept moving him out of their classes because he was simply too advanced. Najee's computer teacher explained to the principal, "Najee knows a *lot* more about computers than I do."

For three difficult months, Najee was moved around. At first he was moved from freshman classes to sophomore classes. Finally, he landed in advanced placement, or AP, classes. As a fourteen-year-old freshman, Najee found himself in some classes with seniors.

Najee has always excelled in academics. Here he is, proudly holding up a Certificate of Achievement from PS 9, back when he was in elementary school.

Najee was struggling to fit in as a normal high school student. Obviously, this was nearly impossible. Smart kids get teased sometimes. Especially a smart kid who is taking AP classes with seniors. "Yeah,"

Najee laughs, "it was tough. I'll bet a lot of kids know what I'm talking about. But I never let it get me down, because I knew where I was headed in life."

Najee was too busy to pay much attention to anything negative. He was trying to juggle a heavy workload at school. He was also still running his computer business. Happily, things settled down by his sophomore year. He was finally able to blend in as an average high school kid. Of course, cool things always seemed to pop up when Najee least expected them. A year later, it would be something else. And this time, it was big—*really* big.

This is the office of "NFTE." It would be a very important part of Najee's future.

Chapter Seven

Awards and Accolades

James, let's check out Spiderman 2 . . . no, Najee, I heard Shrek 2 is funny . . . what are we, ten years old? . . . yeah, Najee, you're right, okay, what time do you want to go? . . . hold on, let me check online . . . all right, it's playing at the Loews theater at 6:00 . . . okay, cool . . . oh, man, was that the bell? Gotta get to class, Najee, text a few other people and see who else wants to go also . . . will do, James, I'll hit you back after school.

After James signed off, Najee switched his Side-kick phone over to e-mail. He e-mailed some of his other friends letting them know about the plans for later. Najee was sitting in the library at Benjamin Banneker Academy during a free period. He usually used the time to read or get some homework done. Reaching into his briefcase, he pulled out the flyer that he had recently come across. Sitting back in his chair, he read it for the third time that day.

The year was 2004 and Najee was in his junior year of high school. He was about to discover a program that would change his life. The flyer was from an organization called NFTE [pronounced "nifty"]. NFTE helped young people move ahead in business and education. Together with a company called Fleet Bank, they were holding a business competition. It was open to any teenager who happened to have his or her own business. The business that showed the most potential to grow would be the winner.

At first, Najee had rejected the idea. What chance would his computer business have in a national competition? Sure, Techmaster Computer Works was doing well and growing. Still, most people would consider it a tiny business. Najee hesitated, but in the end, he decided to sign up for the contest.

In the first round, the judges eliminated everyone other than the top twenty-five competitors. Najee was pleased to be included in this group. Getting in the final twenty-five was a great accomplishment. The judges then narrowed the field down to the top seven. Najee found himself in *that* exclusive group. He couldn't believe it. Things were definitely starting to heat up.

Each of the seven finalists was required to give a speech to the judges. The purpose was to explain what their business did, and how it had room to grow. When it was Najee's turn, he was extremely nervous. "I barely remember what I said," he recalls. "I told them about my background, working on computers and Web sites. I also talked about the potential my business had in New York City—Brooklyn, in particular."

After his speech, Najee answered questions from the judges. His nerves had gone away and he was speaking with confidence. When it was over, Najee had a positive feeling. "I did pretty well," he told his parents later that evening.

This turned out to be an understatement. Najee was announced as the *winner* of the competition. He was shocked. Everyone had always known that he was a smart kid with a lot of potential. Now, things were starting to fall into place.

As soon as Najee won the business competition, things started happening. Here he is attending the "Inner City 100" awards, posing with Kwame M. Kilpatrick, the mayor of Detroit.

Najee was thrilled to collect a large cash prize for winning. More importantly, he found that doors were opening up for him. Over the next two years, he received many awards and accolades. He was invited to attend business meetings in cities such as Washington and Dallas. Najee even went to England! He remembers how cool it was to sit in a fancy restaurant in London. He thought to himself that this was the good life.

Going to different events gave Najee the chance to meet some famous people. For example, he attended an event that included a special luncheon. After everyone had eaten, some celebrities made speeches. One of the speakers was Keyshawn Johnson. He is a famous wide receiver who started his career with the New York Jets. He has also played for the Tampa Bay Buccaneers, the Dallas Cowboys, and the Carolina Panthers.

Keyshawn is obviously a great football player. He's also done some terrific things *off* the football field. Keyshawn had risen up from a poor neighborhood in south central Los Angeles. In his speech, he talked about growing up in a tough neighborhood. It wasn't easy—even for a kid with lots of talent. He had seen other talented young people waste their lives. That gave him the determination to fight twice as hard to make it.

Even after Keyshawn had become famous, he often went back to visit his old neighborhood. He explained that things never seemed to change there. People were still poor, and no buildings or new businesses were springing up. However, now he had the power to do something about it. He convinced other athletes and business leaders to invest money. Conditions in south central Los Angeles started to improve. In his speech, Keyshawn said that it's important to give back to the community.

Keyshawn Johnson with Najee and other young people attending the luncheon.

Najee was listening carefully. Keyshawn talked about ending the violence in the inner city. He said that successful businesses could bring hope. If they were owned and operated by African Americans, that would be even better. Young people wouldn't turn to drugs and crime if they had better opportunities.

Najee thought about his own community in Brooklyn. He realized that he had seen a considerable amount of wasted talent also. Something occurred to him. If he became successful, he could do some of the things Keyshawn was doing. Najee would have the power to put his energy toward helping his community grow stronger. This gave Najee a sense of responsibility. He wasn't doing it only for himself and his family any longer.

Later, after the luncheon was finished, everybody stuck around and chatted. Najee was getting ready to leave when a giant figure approached him. It was Keyshawn Johnson! He was making a point of saying hello to the young people in attendance. "Nice to meet you, Najee," Keyshawn said, flashing his famous smile. "I'm glad you came to a positive event like this one."

"Thanks, Keyshawn. I really respect what you're all about." Najee knew that he was shaking the hand of a person who was a one-in-a-million. Like most kids, Najee had always loved sports. However, he knew that he wasn't going to be a professional athlete. It wasn't because he had no talent. On the contrary, Najee was a good athlete. He had competed in tennis, soccer, and track and field. But Najee was aware that the odds of being a superstar were less than one in a million. He had a much better chance of being successful outside of sports.

Najee, a good athlete, plays many different sports.

Najee respected Keyshawn for making the most of his potential and achieving his goals. Najee, on the other hand, didn't want to focus all his attention on sports. Without question, his gift was his brilliant and creative mind. He was making the most of *his* potential—by playing chess, building computers, and starting a business. This would give him a chance to make a difference in the world.

Speaking to Keyshawn was an inspirational moment in Najee's life. Here he was, standing next to a famous athlete who was also a special person. Yet, Keyshawn Johnson was *also* standing next to a special person: a teenager that cared about education and community, and had avoided the temptations of the street. Najee McGreen was headed for a big future.

Chapter Eight

Making it Big

Saying goodbye is never easy. Najee and his parents were standing in a small dorm room at Johns Hopkins University. This prestigious college is located in Baltimore, Maryland. Here, 200 miles from his home in Brooklyn, Najee was ready to begin college. His mother tried not to cry as she gave him one last hug. Then she and Mr. McGreen left, closing the door behind them.

In the spring of 2005, Najee had graduated from high school a year early. He was only seventeen years old. Many people had been surprised to hear that he would be attending Johns Hopkins. The school was best known for its medical program. Najee's background was in computer science. Everyone thought that he would continue moving along with business and technology.

Najee still loved business and computers, of

course. But he had come to an important conclusion: he could have a bigger impact on the world by pursuing the field of medicine. Three years earlier, upon graduating from middle school, Najee had received a cool gift. His mentor, Mr. Goldhirsch, had given him a book titled *The History of Doctors*. Najee often looked through the book during his free time. He was fascinated by it.

Najee talks about how he was drawn to the idea of combining technology with medicine. "Growing up, I wondered how computers could be used to help people. Then I became interested in medicine. I came to Johns Hopkins to find out how to combine these two fields of study . . . how to get them to work together, and benefit mankind."

There's no way of knowing what might spring from Najee's creative mind. He might end up working with other doctors to discover cures for diseases. He might also use computer technology to figure out new ways of performing surgery. Medicine, like Legos, chess, and computers, is another puzzle for Najee to solve.

For now, Najee stood in his dorm room and took a deep breath. He unpacked his things—a chess set, naturally, among them. He wondered who his new roommate would be. Hopefully, he'd be the kind of guy that might enjoy a few late-night games of chess. Najee stared at the board and smiled. Chess had certainly led him to some pretty amazing places.

Najee's freshman year at college turned out to be the best experience of his life. He made several new friends and was introduced to a world of new ideas. He also received an invitation to attend an important conference. It was called the State of the Black Union 2006.

It had all started almost a year earlier, in May of 2005. At that time, Najee had traveled to Dallas, where he had won yet *another* award.

This is a magazine for the Black Enterprise Entrepreneurs Conference, which was held in Dallas, in 2005.

As though winning the award wasn't enough, Najee received a further honor. Talk-show host Tavis Smiley was organizing the State of the Black Union 2006. Mr. Smiley, a bestselling author and public speaker, was also hosting it. He extended an offer: would Najee like to come, participate, and actually speak at the conference?

The answer was yes. Taking part in this prestigious conference was something Najee was excited about. He thought about great black leaders of the past, and how they had changed America. Najee felt a strong sense of appreciation for the sacrifices these men and women had made—and a responsibility to do his small part in continuing their important work.

Najee in a group photo taken at the State of the Black Union 2006. To Najee's left is the host and organizer of the event, Tavis Smiley.

In February of 2006, Najee and his father traveled to Houston. That was the site of the State of the Black Union 2006. The experience was remarkable. Najee had the opportunity to meet and interact with influential African American leaders. There was a huge luncheon and other events. Najee did a tremendous job, impressing everyone with his intelligence and ambition.

These days, when Najee finds the time, he comes home to Brooklyn. He enjoys hanging out with his family and friends. Najee has been a chess champion, a computer whiz, and a business owner. Now he's a college student.

But Najee has added one *more* thing to the list: chess coach. What makes it so cool is that one of his students lives in the same house. Jabari McGreen is now thirteen years old. He shows as much promise as Najee did at that age. Further down the road, the chess world may discover another McGreen . . . actually, *two* of them! Who knows what twin sisters Maya and Mariah McGreen, age seven, may accomplish.

Najee teaching chess.

As for Najee McGreen, his exciting journey continues. It was just getting underway in 1993. Bill Clinton was the president and *Jurassic Park* was the top movie of the year. That's when a chessboard was placed in front of Najee for the first time. Since then, the New York City skyline has shifted. There have been advances in technology, sports, and business. Of course, New York, as well as America, has never changed more than it did on September 11, 2001.

Najee knows that the world will continue to change around him. He is dedicated to being a big part of that change. It may be fighting diseases as a doctor, or inventing new technologies using computers. No matter what, Najee will surely succeed. He plans to be a positive force in the coming years. He'll do what he can to make this world a better place. That's the ultimate in *making it big*.

Najee believes that making it big is possible for anyone—even young people who may have already made some bad choices in life. He knows that it's not too late for them. Anybody can turn things around and get back on the right track. His hope is that everyone will realize that a bright and happy future is within reach. It's out there for anyone who works hard and stays focused on making *all the right moves* . . . just like Najee McGreen.

Najee's view from the Brooklyn Bridge: bright lights of opportunity.